Dedicated to my mother, Pamela McPhail, who always believed I would be the best no matter what I did, and to my father, L.D. McPhail, who always believed I would do my best no matter what I did. I miss you both every day.

May 12, 2020
Vernon, New Jersey

# Dream Jobs: Getting Started as a Travel Photographer

**by**

## Lawrence E. McPhail

ISBN: 978-1-7350637-1-3 PRINT

# TABLE OF CONTENTS

# Dream Jobs:
# Getting Started as a Travel Photographer

Imagine traveling to beautiful and exciting destinations all around the world, trying delicious food, meeting interesting people, and seeing some of the best views that nature has to offer. Imagine taking photos of everything you see and making money from the entire adventure. And imagine even getting paid to travel by the person who hires you to go there.

Maybe you take a few photos of your morning coffee and sunrise, next you video the locals in a special parade, then later you get invited to watch someone's grandmother make mole - and sample the results, of course. Next week you are going on a river cruise of the Amazon, and you are already planning your great Alaska adventure.

The great thing is that it is all paid for by your travel photographer business. Due to amazing digital technology, it is entirely possible for one person to run a profitable and exciting travel photography business these days. You just need to understand how it works, whether it is for you, and how to make money.

# What Is Travel Photography?

Basically, a travel photographer's job is to take photos and videos that record the things that make an area unique, or to travel for an event that they are contracted to photograph such as a game, graduation, or a wedding.

For example, on any given gig you will take pictures of various landscapes, the people, note how the culture is different, the customs that they have, and their unique history. You can depict all of this in your photography. Anyone who documents a local area or agrees to travel to a location-based photo or video shoot is a travel – or traveling – photographer.

## Travel Photography for Pros and Amateurs

The genre of travel photography is popular with both amateur and professional alike, with much inspiration derived from magazines such as National Geographic with their photographers like Steve McCurry and Renan Ozturk. Steve McCurry's most famous photo was made while reporting on the war in Afghanistan, and his photograph entitled "Afghan Girl" appeared on the cover of National Geographic in 1984.

You can travel and take pictures while traveling, or you can travel to a location to take pictures or video of something specific like a religious ceremony or another event.

## Wide Flexibility

Travel photography can translate into many format styles of documentary photography. Most shooting will be under natural conditions with ambient lighting of a wide variety of indoor and outdoor subjects. Landscapes, people, culture, customs, fun and emotional events, and history are what the photographer frames as his or her subjects. On the commercial side, tourist attractions, hotels, resorts, or anything to do with merchandising travel will often be the topics.

## Wide Range of Skills

Travel photographers must possess a wide spectrum of photographic skills because of the wide variety of subject matter, encompassing not only portraits and landscapes but also wildlife and architectural, and may even include news and event reporting. One day you may be taking pictures of mountain scenery and the next food at a five-star restaurant.

As a travel photographer, you need the necessary skills to photograph basically everything. Patience is essential as well as being well versed in the technical aspects of shutter speed, depth of field, and lighting.

## Tourism - a Driving Force

Travel photography has been popular with tourists ever since cameras were built for amateurs. The famous Kodak Brownie introduced the concept of the snapshot and was very portable. Now with the advent of smartphones and powerful digital cameras, photography is more convenient than ever. Many tourist attractions today are placed in photogenic areas to entice the public to come and take pictures.

## Destination Events

Due to the love of travel, there are more destination events than ever before. Because of that, there is more call for photographers who will travel to locations for those events. If you're willing to do that, you can also schedule extra time before and after any event you are supposed to take pictures at so that you can enjoy the local sites on your own - and yes, photograph them for sale elsewhere.

## Pros Look in More Places

While popular with amateurs taking selfies, the tourist site is not where the professionals usually want to concentrate their efforts. Serious photographers want to capture a sense of culture with an image that conveys a story. Also, a photo of that nature is more marketable for the professional.

## Choose the Unbeaten Path

A pro researches the destination and looks for the unbeaten path that a normal travel agency might not point out to most travelers. A pro does not go through all that effort just to get the "cliché" shots that every tourist with a smartphone gets. A pro wants portraits of the local people, the culture, and interesting or unusual subjects, photos that you cannot get anywhere else.

Many times, pros will use themselves or a traveling companion as their subject but not in a "selfie" manner. A pro wants to analyze a scene and critique it in their mind, work with the composition, lighting, and subject, keeping in mind where the photo might be used. A pro asks herself how a great shot can be made better.

## Be Friendly

People of different cultures are a big part of what travel photographers try to capture. The photographer will want to try to befriend and engage the locals and build connections, with the chance of gaining ideas and locations to shoot. Having a friendly rapport will help people open up to you and perhaps gain you friends who will make the trip even more rewarding.

Travel photography requires that you not only have photographic skills, but also the ability to communicate with people to make them feel comfortable and trusting. Business and marketing skills are needed, too. This means that a person who wants to be a travel photographer needs to be well-rounded in their knowledge. But do not let that scare you away; there is not anything involved that you cannot learn.

# Do You Have What It Takes?

Are you the kind of person that can be a travel photographer? Some people find it is not right for them, while others call it living their dream. If you have ever wanted to travel the world with your camera and make a living at it, this may be the perfect job for you. You still need to carefully consider what the job involves.

You can find many websites glorifying the image of a travel photographer, giving you a lot of superlatives and implying that all kinds of businesses are clamoring for shots, while not offering much information about the real-life commitments required to make a living doing photography of any kind, let alone travel photography. And if you do not already know how to use your camera, there is a big learning curve. It is certainly possible if you really want to do it and are committed to learning the things you need to know about your camera, the market, and business.

## Going from Hobbyist to Pro

Practically everyone starts doing photography as a hobby, a part-time job, or a side gig. Going pro on a full-time basis is a huge leap of faith. It is not a case of just learning how to make good photos that people want, there is also the issue of being able to make enough money to survive doing it. Some may forgo trying to make more money but instead take work to gain experience and network for more prospects, until they can earn enough to at least meet their basic needs. And there is nothing wrong with doing it as side work while you learn and earn. If you love travel anyway, adding "travel photographer" to your resumé when you are taking a cruise or visiting a country is not a huge leap.

## May Require Some Sacrifice

You may have to sacrifice time with loved ones if you are married. A working spouse will gain you some economic stability, but if both spouses work independently, you can do it together even if it will be riskier financially. While you can be somewhat flexible, most photographers understand that there are certain times of the day that are more conducive to good natural lighting.

You will be at the mercy of the time of an event or the weather, usually with no recovery time for jet lag or unforeseen delays in travel. This means you will be tired on the job and may miss opportunities to eat, so you also need to be willing to go hungry sometimes. Pack snacks just in case. Above all, you must be patient.

You will be in situations that are not under your control. Be ready and waiting even if everyone else is not, but you can't expect anyone else to wait on you. You must be prepared to capture any moment, especially if doing event recording.

## You Need Planning Skills

When you have been doing travel photography for a while, you will learn how to plan. Each new place you visit will bring new challenges and you will be dealing with the learning curve again. The trick to succeeding in this profession is planning efficiently, early, and often. You will want to use your time wisely enough to complete the job and still have time to recharge or unwind and enjoy the locations you get to visit.

Once you arrive at your destination, you should hit the ground running, quickly complete any tasks you can as quickly as you can to get them out of the way. You will want to free up whatever time you may have available to explore for yourself while you travel, assuming that was one of the perks of the job that appealed to you in the first place. If the weather is cooperating, use it now instead of waiting until tomorrow. If it keeps cooperating, use it again tomorrow.

Finally, you must never ever get tired of traveling or else you will be tired of your business, your career. There are ways to avoid burn out, such as planning extra time on each trip to recover from traveling and to enjoy some free time. If you are willing to learn photography and business and you don't mind living out of a hotel or on a cruise ship, you may be the next great travel photographer.

# Can You Make a Living from It?

The short answer is yes, you can make a living being a travel photographer, but not everyone can make a living being a travel photographer. You must find the right niche and be willing to think outside the box about ways to sell your work. You cannot get tied up in how things are "traditionally" done. Things are different now with high-speed internet and super-powerful cameras, even on smartphones.

## Stand Out by Being Good

The competition among travel photographers has driven earnings down, which makes some professionals claim that, as a traditional career, travel photography is dying. There are still people working in the field but they only seem to survive and not thrive to the level they think they should. There is an exception, though. If you think of this differently in terms of business and what your audience wants from your photography you may find a fantastic opening to tap into an unlimited income: Be a travel writer.

## Writers Supplement with Their Own Images

If you can write, you can supplement your photography income by blogging about the places you travel to while you share your photography. Many writers turn to photography to support their articles due to the high cost of stock photography or instead of having to pay a photographer for images to accompany their writing. When it comes to the travel industry, having the additional skill of writing will add to your bottom line. That is something the professionals can add on to make additional sales into new markets and publications.

## Travel Expenses

One of the requirements of travel photography is of course travel, which obviously costs money. Some photographers are always on the move going all over the world. They sacrifice home ownership and all the responsibility that comes with it. Why pay someone to mow your lawn when you are going to be in a hotel on the beach, in a chalet in the Swiss Alps, or on a cruise ship in the Caribbean?

You can find many travel vloggers (video bloggers) who often use vlogging, blogging, and travel photography as their sole sources of income. They often report spending, on average, about $2000 a month traveling, which includes meals, accommodations, and general mundane items. The travel photographer who wants to make a good living will likely investigate several sources of income to stave off shortages of work in any area.

## Traditional Newspapers and Magazines

Traditional work such as with magazines and newspapers are not in all that much demand, although some have managed to get a long-term travel photography contract and sell thousands of image licenses to them. It is something that you can investigate that will supplement your bottom line nicely.

Spending a large portion of your time marketing your work is going to be a necessity. You can outsource some of this once you have an income, but until then you will have to spend time marketing your business. One thing to do is to choose the income sources you want to pursue, set up a marketing strategy, and then get started.

You can create multiple streams of income by teaching, selling stock photography, client-direct sales, leveraging social media, blogging, and using YouTube to create a six-figure business if you plan it realistically and are patient.

## YouTube Travel Channels

There are several people with their own YouTube travel channels with thousands of subscribers. A channel with about 5,000 subscribers can earn around $125 per month. Having a travel photography website can do some of the hard work getting your product to market. Utilizing social media and honing your negotiating skills is as key to success as your photo equipment.

## Build Up a Large Stock

Learning to market to advertisers and to seek out buyers of your images will probably occupy a great deal of time. It will help to build up a large stock of images. Get out, go everywhere and start shooting everything. Upload some of your best photos to sites like 500px (https://web.500px.com/), where you can offer your images for licensing. With a stockpile of photos, you will have something on hand to sell. You will also have something to place on your social media as examples and on your web pages for advertising.

Regardless of how well other people are doing or not doing, there is a demand for travel photographers who are willing to be freelancers and find their own opportunities. You do not have to wait for a client to tell you what to take pictures of. You can travel to any destination you want (even close to home) and start taking travel photos now so that you can start building your portfolio and business plan.

# What Skills and Training Do You Need?

The interesting thing about travel photography is that while you do need some basic skills, you do not really have to know everything to get started. What it does require is a long-term commitment to continuously learn about your equipment and craft. There honestly will never be a day that goes by when you cannot learn something new about photography.

## It Requires Training and Dedication

For some people, becoming successful as a travel photographer comes quickly as they are naturals at photography. However, you do not need to rely on natural talent. Instead, you can depend on dedication, effort, and education to master the profession. A diverse set of skills are needed to be a travel photographer, such as the fundamentals of photography based on the type of pictures you want to take, plus business and marketing skills. And of course, a certain measure of bullheadedness and determination.

Some photographers specialize in areas specific to travel photography such as travel portraits, landscapes, or documentaries but they are still skilled in shooting all aspects of photography so they can capture what their audience wants.

## Planning and Research Skills

A lot of time will be devoted to doing research about the places and destinations you cover. Knowing where to find resources and information for your research and planning is a key part of the travel photography business.

For example, you will need to know the type of travel gear and photography equipment you need to pack and what documents you need to fill out before you can work in certain foreign countries.

## Know the Territory

Before you start your travels, you will need an understanding of the history and customs that make the area you are visiting interesting for your photographs. People skills are needed even if your subjects are not human. You will still need to navigate the area and ask questions that will help you facilitate working in the field.

## Note Taking

The ability to take notes about things like your first impressions and how you feel about the destination after you arrive will help you develop your creative instincts for composing shots. Being able to transcribe not just the observational senses but all senses and emotions will be a factor in what you bring to the camera and to your presentations. Those are just a few of the skills needed to succeed in storytelling through your photos.

## Know the Hardware

Digital cameras are packed with features that you are going to want to master. Study the manual to learn how to set the appropriate settings that the conditions and subjects demand. Then after the camera is mastered, the software you will use to organize and edit on the computer will have to be learned as well. If you plan to make money from your first trip, you probably want to ensure you know how to use everything, including the editing software you have chosen.

## Try Some Training

The real test comes in mastering the principles of how you compose a photograph. There are online courses and blogs especially for training in the field of travel photography which are low enough in price to take, just to get your feet wet.

Some of the courses will also train you on how to market your work and how to cover the costs of running your own photography business. Also, they may help you develop a portfolio to get you started. So, investigate some of the available classes online if you feel unsure.

The critical factor here is that you identify gaps in your knowledge or skill so you can find the training you need to fill that gap. The training can be paid or free, the important thing is to learn what you need to know, whether it's the camera, the editing software, marketing education, or learning to travel inexpensively, you have to get the training you need to succeed.

# Where and How to Market Your Photography

This is an exciting aspect of travel photography. Okay, the traveling is impressive too. But making money so that you can keep traveling is even better, right? That is why you need to learn how and where to market your photography. If you are not selling your products, you won't make money no matter how many pictures you take. Getting the images that capture the essence, the stories, and the emotions of the destinations is only part of the task of travel photography when you are in it to make a living.

Somehow all those pictures must be converted to money so that you can at least fly back home. Many photographers may not be under contract, and all those traveling expenses are out of their own pocket. But no worries, it can be done.

## Big Business of the Travel Industry

Commercial travel photography is a huge industry, globally worth around $1 trillion. Advertising by travel agencies, resorts, hotels, and tourist attractions is usually done with imagery, so naturally, there will be a demand for photographers. Merchandising prints and postcards are also big markets for the industry. Having contracts with multiple travel agencies will allow you to sell thousands of image licenses for years. They may even pay for your trips.

## Advertise Yourself

To get more exposure, put some of your work online for display or upload to stock photography sites such as Alamy, Adobe Stock, Crestock, Etsy, Shutterstock, 500px or any other place that suits your needs. Check their requirements and terms of service, so you know how you will get paid.

## Educate Yourself about Your Audience

Today the market arena is the Internet spanning the world, global in scope as far as sales go. Gaining information about who buys photographs, what kind of people are in need of your work, where they may live, and what appeals the most to them will allow you to generate leads for potential customers. Create a tailored mailing list considering all forms of clientele to enable you to find art directors and editors who give out travel assignments.

## Stand Out among the Competition

There is plenty of competition in the photography market. Hundreds of thousands of students every year are getting into the field to begin careers. Working to stand out among the crowd means having your own style and bringing out the emotion attached to the subject of your images. When a publisher is putting together an article on a subject, they may select your photos because they fit the mood or conjure up an emotional connection to the described scene. When you understand what the audience is looking for, you can stand out.

## Get Your Portfolio Ready

One thing you need to do to stand out is to generate a portfolio that identifies you as an accomplished professional photographer. When meeting with prospective clients, your portfolio must contain your best image examples with competent editing that is thoughtfully arranged to hold the attention of whoever looks at it. Your portfolio should be on your own website with a business-like domain name and a professional hosting service. Do not be cheap about your site!

## Start Your Own Stock Site

One way to make money with your travel photography is to start your own stock photo site. Charge a membership fee and let the members use your photos in their work with specific rules and conditions that you set.

## Start a YouTube Channel

Another way a lot of travel photographers make money is via a YouTube channel. But do not worry, you do not have to do a YouTube video where you talk or are the "personality." You can literally put up your pictures with relaxing music and still earn money. Plus if you provide all the right information about licensing the channel will act as a traffic generator to your website.

Making money from travel photography does not have to be done in the standard way of taking a photo and selling the picture. It can look more like taking video, taking photos, and then combining them in different ways to make money. You can make money via a YouTube channel by selling stock photos, by being paid directly for your photos, and more.

# The Importance of Understanding the Local Culture and Language

You do not have to learn every part of every language before you visit countries that do not speak your native language. However, it is a good idea if you at least study the culture a little bit, plus learn a few important phrases based on your normal needs when you travel. Do not forget that you can also use technology to help. With such resources as Google Translate available to everyone with a smartphone, you are going to be just fine.

## Find Resources to Pick Up the Culture

Go to the library and research travel books and find brochures from a travel agency, or better yet, make friends with a local travel adviser. Remember, they are paid by travel suppliers, not by the people who use them to arrange travel, so they do not mind talking about some of the "tricks of the trade." They can often put you in touch with people who have been to a destination you are considering so you can get first-hand information. Knowing the culture of your destination is important. You want to be able to smoothly traverse the area in a manner that does not draw attention to yourself. Get into the habit of working with the same travel adviser to plan and prepare all your travel, they can develop a profile for you that makes quick trips and short deadline travel a lot easier and more successful, and they may be able to market some of your work as well. A good travel agent can make your job a little easier and maybe even a little more profitable.

## Blend in and Don't Be the Distraction

Try to blend in to make yourself less noticeable to the locals. You want them to be the subject of your images and catch them behaving naturally, as if you were not there. To be less noticeable may require that you to be able to converse in their language, at least to some extent. Learn common phrases for asking directions, how to order in restaurants, direct cab drivers and exchange pleasantries.

One key phrase to remember is how to say, "Can I take your picture?" In many countries, you can get by in English if you at least try. For example, in many European countries you can get by with only speaking English because many people there can converse in it, but they will respect you more if you try to speak their language. Even if you butcher the language, they will still appreciate it if you make the effort.

## Find an Online Language Course

There are a few online language instructors to get you started, as well as plenty of YouTube channels to gauge how well your understanding has progressed. Things like learning the Spanish alphabet can be learned from Sesame Street videos. You cannot learn it overnight, though, so give yourself plenty of time. You might also try something like italki.com where you can learn to speak any language naturally (https://www.italki.com/home).

It is never too early to start. The more you know the language, the less you will have to rely on interpreters or guides, which may save you some money. While learning the language, you will often pick up some of the customs and some of the culture as well. Some are easier to learn than others, with the Asian languages and cultures often being among the hardest to pick up.

## Show Respect

Most people know to take off their shoes when entering a temple, and if it is frequented by tourists, there will often be signs in English to remind you. You should remember to also do so at anyone's home you visit.

Be aware that you are not to step or stand or sit on the raised threshold at the entrance of a temple; always walk over the threshold without touching it. When it comes to cameras, some temples allow photography while others expressly forbid it. Be aware of the local customs before you go anyplace so that you can show the proper respect.

Ask permission before bringing your camera into view. In Indian temples, there may be a strict dress code to which you will have to adhere to enter. As with any culture, the more you become familiar with the traditions and customs, the easier it will be for you to get around to accomplish the job and perhaps help you enjoy the profession.

In many foreign countries, you do not want to do something and ask forgiveness later because that could end up with you being at odds with the law. Instead, ask before you do anything and always learn the customs before going.

# Travel Photographer Business Tips

A travel photographer has a multifaceted business that has a lot of income streams available. You need to be able to take good photos, keep them organized, and offer them in the right sizes and formats that your audience needs for their use. You must also understand who your audience is and how to get your product - the photos and videos - in front of them so they can make a purchase.

## Invest Wisely

To run a business, it is best to learn good entrepreneurial practices. Do not invest too much money or time until you know you can be profitable. Never bite off more than you can chew. Try to find nearby projects that will help with gaining photography experience and help you build a portfolio without breaking the bank.

Stick with the common-sense business practices and invest only what you can afford so you stay comfortably afloat. For example, only use a less expensive camera to start out instead of the top of the line camera.

Even if you can afford the top of the line, buy something less expensive until you figure out all the risks of the profession. Losing or ruining a cheaper camera is not as catastrophic to the budget and will help you keep on going.

## Start Locally to Save On Travel

Start in your hometown and eventually work further into the country. When enough capital has been built up from domestic work, go for overseas travel. Start with photographing places you would like to visit that interest you the most and just shoot a lot of pictures. Remember that to others, your home area may be an interesting travel destination.

## Shop for Price

Find out how to shop for trains, planes, and hotel fares. Keep in mind that the less money you spend on travel, the more money you earn. When starting out, just go out locally and shoot digital photos to build your portfolio. Start licensing the photos to stock photo sites on the Internet to get yourself into the market. Make sure that whenever you travel, you treat it as an opportunity to build your portfolio, even if that's not the primary reason for your travel.

## Try Exchanging Services and Promote Expertise

Try bartering images for services like lodging at a resort. You are merely trying to advertise your product in the early stages. Once you are established, you can name your price. Clearly define your area of expertise and know how to express your qualifications with accuracy and confidence. A potential client will want to know about what your specific skill set entails. The name of the game is to get out and find business and sell yourself.

## Network

Offer your photographic services to every travel or tourist business in your current area. Design a logo for your company. Make it memorable but straightforward, less than three colors is usually a good idea to keep production and printing costs down. Use services like VistaPrint that help you design your logo and print it on cards and advertising pieces, and when you are happy with the look of your logo, have a professional create a website to sell your images and present your portfolio.

Do not skimp here and put any cheap site up. Either study long and hard on how to put one up yourself, or have it done by an experienced pro. Then keep working on marketing yourself by engaging in social networking, in-person networking, and generally getting your name out there.

## Use Social Media

Join a few social groups and participate in their forums and groups that are in common with your field of photography. Members may know where work is available and might be willing to convey that knowledge to you. You may also be able to ascertain what you can charge for your services by seeing what your contemporaries are getting for theirs from the forums or the photographer websites that they have. Like any good business, the key is understanding how others succeed and figuring out how that can work for you. Then, fill in the gaps and make it better.

## To Sum Up

Your travel photography business can succeed and make money. The most important thing is to get started ... and get started with the right information. Understand that you need to know how to take good photos and put them in the correct format for your buyers to use. You need to know how to travel to places safely and affordably, navigate the area, communicate with the local, and the ultimately take the best photos with an idea in mind of who will buy them. And have fun doing it!

www.ingramcontent.com/pod-product-compliance
Lightning Source LLC
LaVergne TN
LVHW050950080826
845145LV00004B/1462

* 9 7 8 1 7 3 5 0 6 3 7 1 3 *